lisan al'asfour

natalie hanna

arp books | winnipeg

ARP Books (Arbeiter Ring Publishing)
205-70 Arthur Street
Winnipeg, Manitoba
Treaty 1 Territory and Historic Métis Nation Homeland
Canada R3B 1G7
arpbooks.org

Cover artwork and design by Leslie Supnet.
Interior layout by Relish New Brand Experience.
Printed and bound in Canada by Imprimerie Gauvin.

Canada Council   Conseil des arts   MANITOBA ARTS COUNCIL
for the Arts   du Canada   CONSEIL DES ARTS DU MANITOBA

Canadä   Manitoba

ARP Books acknowledges the generous support of the Manitoba Arts Council
and the Canada Council for the Arts for our publishing program. We acknowledge
the financial support of the Government of Canada and the Province of Manitoba
through the Book Publishing Tax Credit and the Book Publisher Marketing
Assistance Program of Manitoba Culture, Heritage, and Tourism.

Library and Archives Canada Cataloguing in Publication

Title: Lisan al'asfour / Natalie Hanna.
Names: Hanna, Natalie, author.
Description: Poems.
Identifiers: Canadiana (print) 20220409633 | Canadiana (ebook) 20220409668 |
    ISBN 9781927886663 (softcover) | ISBN 9781927886670 (ebook)
Classification: LCC PS8565.A579 L57 2022 | DDC C811/.54—dc23

MIX
Paper
FSC   FSC® C100212
www.fsc.org

contents

dawn, unfold
your body like a love emerging
from the blanketed hollow
of the bed and
in the first moment glow
a little on my face and arms
that i may remember
i am wanted

in my sweetest dreams i am still stealing flowers
from every public bush, a menace to marigolds
armed with pruning shears, escaping at speed
with armfuls of lilacs, dianthus, and snapdragons
the bittersweet nightshade grown to monstrous size
drooping over branches of petal-dropping
apple blossom and magnolia
a riot of iris spears strangled with myrtle
i am not above sneaking through
the gardens of the very posh neighbours
to carry off the peonies, for what do i care
for the worries of ants and the sleepy bees
when i too am so empty of honey

pharmacognosy papyri came to
rest around the world

i cradle the compendium
of herbs and wildflowers
from my mother
who tells me that even within
the same garden one plant
among its sisters may grow mean
and full of poison for lack
of water, lack of sun
lack of goodness from the earth

the rosewater that sings
love into my mouth
is but a diluted breath
of grandmothers' arias
distilling rose oil
so strong that one drop
would soothe a baby's colic
and two drops be
the last lullabye

anemone

spears
        of
        underwater light

show hands   maybe mine

reaching past
my
        ink cloud

                hair

to drown words

            unleashed freely

where sound
            no longer
carries

            it is hard to be truly clean —

on surfacing
                feet gather sand
            the body magnet of detritus
an enemy, an enemy

how different i feel
console me

i close the night inside me

                    behind my eyes
        galaxies created by the pressure
                        of my hands

do not stand up as a witness against me

kin, how do we speak? does the sound arising
from our mouths reach ears with nostalgia or
with pique, suck sucking teeth, tongue between
gaps. how do we speak? hand in open position
asking for yours, hand on my shoulder, a kiss
on each cheek at each hello. how too we speak:
screams erupting in flocks from branches, we
learning serial phrases, cautious as words plunge
into the pit between songs of celebration. beloveds
how we too speak, posture of rest, posture of
cooking, cup of tea on saucer extended. open
your mouth! show me what flaps about inside: the
want, the trap of simple joys held onto forever
in case we are never rich enough to taste them
again, let laughter testify in favour of our continued
existence as much as the dichotomy of mended seams
and fine silk, the stitched together syntax
of needlepoints so vast we could step inside
run away forever from all sorrows, for
we speak in the meter of doubt. we speak fear
by question: what is the life of each of us worth?
we speak in thanks and apprehension
by the grammar of eyes counting children's heads
in the yard. my kin, my heart, do not stand up
as a witness against me — when we step into the next life
what sound will our speech leave behind?

naharda[1]

her singing voice wakes me
sets the table
her voice, the library of alexandria
drives the sun across the whole sky
i know only her voice and within its resonance i am made to rise

                                        out reach i and
                            hands little sandy my with
                              face mother's my kiss to
              television the at wave to hands reach i and
teaching both of us, mama and me, english words
english that begins to swallow us
whole, i forget how to say *today*
in arabic, always *yesterday*
and sometimes *tomorrow*
as the sound of her singing
me rhymes for children
in her mother tongue
fades   garden the in sit i
                                        seed of full hands
                                    there placed has she
                                asafeer 'il awaiting
                        perches their from down fly to
            song their of secret the me teach and
i fetch from time with thin halawa ears
the intonation used to call children to meal
kolli ya habibti, kolli —
a bird pays no mind
to whether the hand that feeds it eats

failure to way gives everything, *bukra*
line her of faces the back call i
voices the not but
song of lack with i am shameful
along get to refusal stubborn and
alone are we though even
other each but fight to one no have

il ingilisi spills out of me like water leaping off a cliff
ya Rab, she says, do you ever stop talking?
i am afraid if i do not fill the universe with words
i will forget language altogether
i have already forgotten one

heard they when askance looked someone, *imbarrih*
accent arabic your

imbarrih i hurt you, correcting your english diction, but
your school-taught colonizer french is perfect
at least three tongues braiding stories in your mouth

english into words arabic translate to you ask i
you, simple so not is it say you
— people a translate to me asking are
sea the across telephone playing like it's

what will happen to us when your first language
is the only one that remains
and we are sliding through your atmosphere
in the abruptness of *what's wrong?*
mish oulini ya om'mi, fi eh?
tell me mother, what's wrong?

script arabic bound-right the forgot i *imbarrih*
hands holding symbols of formed is read cannot i
side either on hands holding am i like
survival for necessary is what with
narharda, i set my own table
naharda, i kiss my mother's face goodnight

notes in the margin of the hospital itinerary

what if i walked away
from the woman warming
the uncooperative veins in my hands
with bags of warm water
and found myself the pair of
arms i've been discounting
to do the job instead

what if i let the pen scribble
across the calendar written over
with appointments for doctors
unable to scry me in
bright cool rooms

what if i filled the hollow
of the womb with sadness
gave birth to it
in the spring grass
to soothe it with
young unfurling leaves

what if i never spoke and
you sang for me instead
in the voice i lost
on the operating table

what if i lifted away
from the table altogether
and never came home like i imagined
before the anaesthesia took effect

body of christ

i smelled it
the overdrive wet cotton candy
the summer hot field
childhood lip glosses
and bubblegum — that sweet
on the edge of the knife
i'd used to trim the greens
from the first strawberry
i ate after surgery

after the moment of
total oblivion
the interstitial rip from
the stale body

weeks of being able
neither to smell nor taste anything
joylessly placed in my mouth
like a lapsed communion wafer
in the canned hospital air

i sat there
turning and smelling the blade
for minutes
afraid i would never
meet it again

wondering why the fruit itself
did not smell as sweet
and whether i could plunge
its bright flower into other flesh
with knife tip

to feel no pain at all

the first mother made the second
in her body, made the other mothers all
daughters of her
many divided nations

some of us disappoint her

i give my body to the women
to cover with sigils of life
with paste made from henna trees

in my skin will bloom
flowers and leaves
the scalloped vines that
bind us together

you hold my hand, dappled burnt sienna
as if a communion wafer
in your holy white palm
apply it your face like armistice

how your strange consolation
fails to bring forth even water
from this body that will not give
of itself anymore

you can hide your mistakes
in the mud, for it
takes time for the pattern to develop —
what we fail to wash off
leaves the longest stain

mothers, don't fret
i will marry myself by the lamplight
and draw the children of the earth
so well upon me that
when i bring the last night
on my hands, smelling of roses
you will scarce know how
much of me remains

magic show

i.

tricky, the foolishness of being glamour ready
and lipstick smooth for this kind of exam
coming straight from work, alone, to mute
my power with the sorrow of other
empty women, or women afraid they will
empty too soon, as they shuffle me around
agree to refer me elsewhere for problems
outside of their scope, into the administrator's office
i was clearly never meant to see, this wall of babies'
smiling faces they ostensibly helped create
through magic they won't perform for me, there's
a reason it's not in the waiting room

ii.

i'm sorry, i'm sorry, your patter repeats
as you force the blades, try six times
with three different duck bills
one, ratchetching plastic
two, it has amused you, to pull from the fridge
but you announce with flourish *the cervix is high*
as though i am a sacrifice that refuses to lay still
as if this act has not been performed
on this body dozens of times
by better-skilled hands
i can just see the tip, just the tip to swab
for diseases i've been checked for already
i'm sorry, you sing
but you brought your tricky cervix today
so i'll stop torturing you —
get dressed, while i clean up here
go on, i won't look
not even a notional shame
escapes you as you leave
the curtains open
to the audience

iii.

yesterday i came home and hung
the chocolate ice cream in a bag
off the frozen garden doorknob
for safekeeping from my feelings

but took pity on its gentle nature
in the afternoon, popped it on
a dining chair while shovelling
the back step clean to exhaustion

in the morning i came down
to the earnest cat
examining the puddle of sweet brown
soup dripping down the formal chair
as if she knew that consolation is poison

iv.

the clinic website advises its guests
not to isolate when dealing with infertility
but the doctor's mouth forms the words

there's a 1–2% chance in a healthy woman
your age, your decaying little eggs
with their weak mitochondria can't power
a pregnancy, confers with her junior
to drive the point home

i exceed acceptable thresholds
and the science of preservation
will not be applied to me but for
the grand ta-da of coming back
80 lbs lighter / 10 years ago

after brown
(for j.fraser)

after your levantine bred grandmother
stands crib-side and says so snide
her skin's too dark, too father-side arab
can't pass for white
to your ivory toned mother

after *don't embarrass us*
with your bad hair, so kinky
god deliver us from shame
can't you do something with it?
straight perms, the clothes iron
after half of it falls out
after i don't hate it anymore

after suspicious glances, after i hear
those backwards people
again on the bus, trance out to loud music
lady, i can still hear you
but i was raised with manners

after *dirty arab, sandn_gger*
come from the mouth of someone you love
or someone you thought you loved at least
after *you exotic beast, after where you from, baby?*
no i mean your family. no i mean originally
fine, be difficult, you're not making friends
available or enemy

after *don't be offended, i didn't mean you*
i don't see your not-whiteness
but you can't say my colour, don't see me at all
after you lift the imprint of offence and
take a hint of my skin up with it each time

after you look in my eyes you say are almonds
and tell me to make your coffee with milk
like the colour of my skin

after *oh, you grew up here*
you're not really arab, like them
like us, like who?

after *what do you think about the arab terror problem?*
i think we are terrified of being called
the arab terror problem

after *say inshallah,* after i do
after *what are you?*
you're not white
not white
after so much is written
on this so much body
to tell it what to think
of what it is and isn't

i meet a young woman one day
who still has her smile
and doesn't shake hands
but opens arms wide and holds me soft
before i even say hello

and says
nice to meet you,
you're brown.
i'm brown too.
what kind of brown are you?
and after brown what are you?

we cry openly at table

i.

little sister, what have we done
we're the last two matryoshka in the family line
i think mother may have liked it if we had made
more storytellers and this is her witchcraft
enticing into being babies to hear
fables of whip-fast great grandmother's
whisky & ice cream bar at
ras-el-bar in summery damietta
or chilling tales of punishments doled
by evil grandmothers
the resulting fear of dark enclosed spaces

ii.

she's learned going forth is never as good:
this obtuse canadian winter that refuses
to befriend her, blights even its own from the streets
her throat singing a persistent siren of otherness
as her weighted tongue works round
inelegant new words and idioms
she works without end for forty years
but ends by ascending three short stairs
to a bed made for giants of old
built by four men, in situ
her reward

iii.

she's learned you can't go home again
by slow exodus of all but the family's old
by the stiff-spined ghosts of lost childhood places
and the well-appointed flats
in metropolitan tahrir square
its mortal flood of fierce once hopeful bodies
now renowned red salvos
a state of emergency of the heart
who are these people, she asks
who take turns killing each other in the streets?
we lived in peace, she says
we lived in peace

iv.

sister, amidst
her gargantuan claustrophobic
rococo and baroque set pieces
that strangle each other for the throne
in her modern airless bungalow
amidst the gilded aubusson chairs
that look like they may walk away
in the manner of wary birds, amongst
these things we come to know her
acquiring and curating strange details
as from time to time discovered

her parents hid from her for years
her own alabastrine beauty, so much royal
that rumour of her spread and popular
designers of the day asked to dress her
in their défilés de mode
it makes me happy, she says,
to think of what my life could
have been, the saddest thing
we have ever heard

married doctors of the golden age

from the angle of my seat
at my mother's favourite restaurant
i can see the busboy scrape
remains of a dish into the bin
before the chef can notice

complicit in hiding a fraught conversation
i drop the eugenides' paperback
into my bag, tucked partly under
the crowded table shivering with glass

what are you reading, my stepfather asks
i run through a list of things not to say, settle for
— *there's a woman from greece who keeps parakeets*

my mother anoints the freshly baked bread
in oil and vinegar as she responds
we used to keep caged canaries in egypt
and wake to their singing each morning

— *we don't brag about animal cruelty,* i want to say
roll eyes, *everything's done different these days*

the seafood platter comes and goes
with the eggplant parm we audition for
my sister's wedding, yet unconceived

stepdad asks, *why are you taking pictures of food?*
hashtag family, hashtag feast

hashtag pasta lethargy
do you know that this is called "octothorpe?"
betting i don't, like daring me to explain
the etymology of the word 'justice' in law school
conspiring with laughter for my quick "*justinian code*" reply

though it's where they held their wedding feast
mother one day will refuse to return here
when the owner's son, so pleasant, so present
pleads guilty to outmoded gangsterism

— *who knows what else he might be bootlegging,* she snorts
and asks for the provenance of her scallops
as impatient hands, corded with muscle
use the rubenesque back of a butterknife
to rend the carapace of steaming lobsters
when the claw crackers fail to appear

now retired they spend their days in the yard
studying peristeronic affairs, *tutting* me regarding
the plight of arab pigeons, stuffed and roasted
believing the cedars full of mourning doves
too paired and pitiful to eat

bird's tongue

ana mish ayza   [i don't want to
akol lisan al'asfour   eat the bird's tongue]

and now wonder
if i had done
would the language   [of my mother's homeland]
have remained

the kindest words
of my softest years
kolli, ya albi   [eat, oh my heart]

i am not lying
no birds
were harmed

don't salt supper
with your tears

a place she keeps clean

he sat at the desk and said he understood
how a man could travel, location to location
kill the women who enraged him

he sat at the desk and said he would kill himself
but first me and everyone else in the building
if i didn't fix the mess he made
said my death was on his head

he sat at the desk where i rest my elbows
and cast curses, defamed my name to god
when i said i was no barracuda

he sat at the desk where i eat my lunch
and removed his clothes
as i told him to stop

he locked me in the room
at the desk where i'm told to stay calm
screaming *dumb bitch* until
a woman in the next room over
hit the panic button and
police busted in

he sat at the desk, said he needed a woman
or two to serve him, tend to his needs
leaned in close and said
damn you smell good

he sat at the desk, and called me a witch
for predicting his problem
by the forms he clutched, as though
he were special and this not my trade

i lept from the desk to throw my body over
the baby as it screamed in the carriage between them
grown men, knuckles out, who couldn't bear to wait

he shrugged at the desk where my
book of photos stayed closed
reminding me without revealing
what i have to live for
said everyone hits each other now and then
followed me out of the building
followed me almost home

index of error

i

say it again, how you want to speak with the lawyer
and *not the receptionist, honey,* how you wonder if
my last name is jewish because you don't do business
with any of *those.* i want to build enough tension
relish the rise from behind my desk —
surprise, the lawyer is me!
and i didn't pay for all that school to be called honey
goodbye, goodbye, get out of this room
let me sweeten it with please
poison it with teeth

ii

oh how you stamp the desk with your palms in just
the right way to make maximal sound erupt between
us, your timid new wife on your side of the desk jumping
like a startled cat before her eyes turn floorward as if
to say sorry, i am sorry. you can call me worse than
hitler all you like, but you're still wrong about the law
and i am not obliged to tremble in your wake

iii

i think we can address the problem here by making
full disclosure of our respective positions in this
touchy situation, for example, i did not anticipate
in medias res, that you would drop your large warm
hand onto my thigh as i was advising
on the tax implications of your monthly payments
and i know legalese is a little off-putting and
you're unfamiliar with the language of rigidity
inter alia, so i will make it clear about
the next thing that happens

iv

not so sure about open spaces, but in the office
she opens her niqab, takes off her gloves to shake my hand
small and interested in compromise. i remember the
first time i met her, walking her back to her average car
to guard against recurrence of a white man screaming
in her direction, *take that off, you're in canada now*
to a woman in canada always, and in canada now
i use my body to shield her body, in canada now
i say the mantra, i am sorry, i am sorry

v.

the young hijabi girls narrow their eyes at me
asking but fearing a protocol breach - *are you arab?*
you're arab, i know, but what kind?
i recite my parents' birthlands
full arab, they say, *but a lawyer, which means*
you were born here like us

this is how they describe the fear
that waits on the pale of limitation

i am lucky, i say, to be driven to study
to have received the education
my mother wrested from hers so bitterly
you understand, you must learn, i say
even when they fight you —

sage and silent nods over the list of still
unasked questions in their hands

peremptory challenge

i.

are you a canadian citizen? have you ever been

ension or pardon? provide your gender:

you have not been granted a record susp

k, read and understand french?

male or femae? do you speak, read

convicted of a criminal offence that can be

i don't quite feel myself
today, they say the truth
lies in our hearts, they say
the truth lies, they say the
truth, they say the truth
lies, they say the truth lies
in our hearts, i don't quite
feel myself today, i don't .

and understand english? do you speak

prosecuted by way of an indictment for which

ii. [2]

the morning tea between us
stepfather asked me
one time, knowing
why do they call it justice?
reaching for
emperor justinian

there is no right of like
though like has come

the heir of a
letterless swineherd
has given us law:

> whose rough
> or polished hands
> grip the codices
> beetle-backed
> wall of scuta?

> what has become
> of the body of law
> of the body by law
> of the bodies?

iii.

to what door
did the summons to duty
come for the man
of no fixed address?

who, his neighbourly peer?

iv.

they say the truth lies in our hearts

i don't quite feel myself today

they say that truth is housed
inside us, but on cross examination
i can't remember where i stood
when the jury was selected
what corner of the room
when the potential justice makers
were summarily excused

a manyness of truths
coming together
and parting, startled fish
in water troubled
by little questions
falling

v. [3]

inside this box, everything
that twelve have ever known
and nothing they have not

> [no heart boxed in
> by the sound of no
> of epithets
> the slander of
> of the drunken slide
> into the river
> the ice
> of the starlight tour
>
> boxed in
> that side
> of the eyelids]

to whom a jury
of snakes?
to whom a jury
of apples?

of those put out of eden?
of those stuck on the ark
in the mounting flood?

there are more things
in heaven and earth
than are dreamt of
in your philosophy

vi[4]

in how many languages
can we ask, are you a citizen
and exclude the first ones?

> [i'm afraid i don't
> understand the question]

on the balance of probabilities
is this body impartial
by answer, demeanour
reactive degree?

peregrine praetor
you might as well be
for your strangeness
with the customs of the land
where you have settled
gripping deep

what mind can tread
deftly between

> *a gun in the hand of (mistaken) righteousness*
> *a gun in the hand of slanted (learned) fear*

vii

a justice of consequence
reclining on
the broken back of mercy
a violence, collateral
doled out to the constellation
of those who have
and have made
suffering

this is the way it works
stop calling it justice
there is no word, no act
can put breath
back in the body

there are some in every crowd

(— written during the ongoing occupation of ottawa, during the COVID *pandemic, february 2022)*[5]

white he, my junior
who professes his love
you say i have it all wrong
i will meet some fine people
down there near the hill
occupying the streets with their trailers
and trucks, diesel fumes destroying
the air at all hours against their
trumpets of armageddon

angel, you sounded so long
you broke your own horn
and tell me now take care
of the media i consume
forget about people calling them racists
i mean, there are always some in every crowd

the whiff of death surrounds us
pan demotic, pan daemonium
as the wild grief builds —
hands wrenched from the grasp
of the honoured elderly and frail
tortured without breath to speak
last wishes, no beloveds
by hospital beds
to match their eyes and witness

white he, i am no longer here to hold you
go look for warmth there
where they burned the canadian flag you adored
crying *freedom! freedom!* while the unmarked graves
of Indigenous children
rise in their thousands across the land

tell me who amongst your fine folks loves
the Charter so well as to know that freedom
is subject to *such reasonable limits*
prescribed by law as can be demonstrably justified
in a free and democratic society

there are many ways to poison the air:
my friends are not free to
walk through choked streets
without the miasma of rage
barking *sheep* into their faces
breaking the back
of the hard-won line
my body my choice

who could it be chasing women in the road
to take off their masks
punching a deacon in the streets
and dancing on the tomb
of the unknown soldier
crying *freedom! freedom!?*

where does your body end
and mine begin? how many cycles
inhalation, exhalation

before we have shared all the air
in this atmosphere with each other
with the neighbourhood
across the earth? what is in you
lives in me, as risky as a kiss

the years i, brown she, lived before you
were not a head start outrunning hate
to some promised land
where none of this could happen —
your freedom is white, your freedom's a man
your freedom is non-disabled and young
and you disavow what your body never lives

in this place where i was born, the confederate
and nazi flags are carried today
on shoulders of those
who don't exist in your books
and raid food from shelters
intended for the bellies of our
neighbours in need

the children, the women, old men, cashiers
whom you might have greeted next door
fetching the morning paper or on your daily rounds
but for an accident of geography
their masks were snatched by ghosts, must be
and the two white faces who set alight
a tenement lobby are unknown to all

it is carnival time for your very fine folks
who have commandeered the local park

and baseball diamond, with food huts
and rides, saunas and weapons —
the party atmosphere lending itself
to jerrycans full of fuel or water
to confuse police, passing in the hands
of smiling john does and janes

freedom! freedom! cried out by soujourners
playing games where the prize is fear if these
unknown wisps can shatter targets of
home and shop windows flying rainbow flags
and shitting in the lovely snow

under the guise, under the guise
of frustrations, white he, that may have been known
by others who are tired and scared
your very fine folk who don't trust the science
sit on a bankroll of vanishing cash
fattened by american dollars passed on
by dirty hands that hate government

their horseback riders waving flags
to rally the southern swell of hate
their mares' noses steaming in the winter air
twenty-five below, some hallucination

while, white he, they swell with self-love
holding residents hostage in their homes
crying *freedom! freedom!* while handcuffs
clasp apartment tower doors

while trailers camp on wellington street
with laundry strung out
and children wearing sandwich boards
play in the dirty snow
as fine folk scream at journos, *get rid of the lies*
while getting rid of evidence
that there are two canadas

know for me, white he
all i would have never wished to know
sift for me, white he, the peaceful
from the hateful, tell me by eye
which are the *always some in every crowd*
on this sardine can train
hustling on the corner, in the masses
police fear will engulf them

do not say you love me and mine —
to lie in mud and stand up clean
the miracle you work, white he
for your kind and no other

the mountains we become while inhabiting the earth

let us talk of the honey we expected
to glaze our lips
by the time we knew the path of the evening sun
so well as to take its glory for granted

let us sing an elegy for embroidered galabeyas
handed down by our mothers
we imagined wearing in the gardens

so tender did we think our limbs would remain
every precious moment of light
illuminating our changeable faces

never knowing it is possible to accrete
stillness over lifetimes such that we bend
to the law of mountains

everything obeys some law —
we didn't know we'd smash tectonic woes
so large into existence
or how the tears would later wear us
how the wind would sand us smooth

where a crevice might occur
we thought to offer water
instead of receive it

now we are mountains and the evening sun
sets on our faces decorated in equal measure
in fragrant cedars and the coloured flags
of adventurers who have made their mark —
ourselves the kind of stoic
taken for hostility

inside we are still posed in dance
fossils in gossamer, thinking how small
and simple were our songs once

but the law of the mountain is greatness
to make fearless longest nights
when we care not what scales our craggy shoulders

offer ruth for the mountain that knows
only catastrophe can undo it

the face of the moon

i.

i caught moon by birth
i caught moon by accident
i caught moon by hot pursuit

am struggling to hold her still
she drags me, sky arms
and ragged feet
across the earth
till, i am tired

face of the moon, mother
calls me
the expectation of brightness
hard to shake

each time i dip my face
in the water to wash
my eyes, moon sees
over my shoulder
ripples, laughing
until just formless light

everyone about her
watching her face
fan dance the month

i am so sick of moon

your failed heroics
we could both see coming
the inevitable physics
of the white water rising
over my head
as your feet came down hard
from the vigorous jump
to erase her

ii.

in the quiet night
as slow i walked
my childhood paths
i heard them

and gaining the hill
where i used to lie
and roll in the grass
breathing smooth

the green blades cool
beneath my head
and thick in my hands
like the fur of vast beasts

the moon broke
the cloudy sky
silvery, gently touching
with relieved familiarity

their many gleaming faces
long dresses and hijabs
in the field below me
in the dark sitting

with children on knees
and blankets laid with food
laughing in the voice
of my beautiful mother

as their boys raced and bragged
and jostled and roared
and their husbands smoked shisha
or prayed in the fieldhouse

as if someone had turned
the switch off on day
as though nothing
could stop them now from living

oil

coconut, olive, and macadamia
shine bright on the surface
of some
soak into me instead

i will never be soft

sometimes in the mirror
i see everything lost
from the time before
i was born

in your mind there is
a land you think is mother

she warns it is the dark water
that will drown you
if you mix yourselves together

she is where you're from, she
tells you there's no need
to get up close to tombs
designed to kill intruders

mother looks at me

i.

post sunday dinner
we gather in the roost
for mother hen's clucking
over ominous coffee grounds
in upturned cups:

something bad will happen

ii.

bad things happen to prodigal young:

mother pounds the prophecy
of who can never be a child of Masr
when they forget to say "Alhamdullilah"
cannot hold their tongues
or know, as sure as sunrise, that only rashwa
makes life move

iii.

bad omens will come to pass, mother enjoys lamenting:

one day she says to her seamstress keening
for a wayward son
this is the price we pay when we come here
we gain the country and lose our children

when it's over
mother looks at me
says as casual as you please
there is nothing arabic in you

iv.

i defend: with all blood kin

i defend: go on listing every food i've ever made
            lay out a feast in words of recipes made by feel
            mother, grandmother, great grandmother taught me
            i am the grape vine leaf
            the spiced meat gently tucked into tender dough
            the syrup poured on sweets by gnarled hands
            so much rice

i defend: jasmine, rosewater, orange
            sumac, hibiscus, and mangoes

i defend: the common dialect stays in my ear
            if not on my stubborn tongue

i defend: white baptismal gown in the desert kinisa
            a sea of black-robed abounas chanting kyries
            as the incense rises in crumbling photos

            the smell of the women
            cooking post-mass lunch
            in the church basement
            endless loaves of holy urbaan
            received with a scarf covering my hair
            a kercheif over my hand

i defend: with those who ask my hair and my skin of their homeland

i defend: the curses heaped on ancestors

i defend: the pressure, the pressure
                   i, too, a bad thing
                   half of what you'd forget

v.

i defend, i defend, i defend, i defend, i defend, i defend, i defend, i defend

am i real? what can i be?
devour all of this
half-knowing shame
am even i forbidden?

softly i say, to soothe mother's rage
that belonging nowhere is a parcel of stone
bestowed on newcomers' children also
words in every alphabet choke in my throat

vi.

mother, how could you think i don't know?
i, pulled apart, cleaving to the shore of your youth
as we root in this land
i, pulled like halawa
until i am thin and dirty

i, who must build a home in my heart
make up for everything lost
make up for all that's denied you

the ultimate sadness of cotton-ball words
in my mouth
i understand now, everything
needs room to breathe

syrian aperture

and did the warplanes come in the early morning as they slept. and it was the chemical bomb that so quick laid children down like lazy piles of cherubim, the eyes surprised and hands upturned, mouths still shaping "holy, holy, holy is the Lord Almighty; the whole earth is full of His glory." and did they choke on the gas of hatred. and their saviours, punched out silhouettes, fell in holy fits of foam as they too drew the air. and their relations rent, so tender were their bodies laid one against the other. and did they seem to peer still out from behind the other's arm. and where they lay them down to rest, holy, holy Lord Almighty, the whole earth weeps, full of glory. ah the eye, the eye, the eye! the dullness of the eye that does not dream. the pupil forever begging light.

white coat
(for razan al-najjar)

one morning in gaza
the world was extinguished
with a rush of air
imploding along with
the voice
calling her name

a bullet pulled
the night neverending
though the camp and
her body

she is empty now
the knowledge
of mending flesh
and courage poured out
of the hole
undammable
unfillable with tears

method of exit

in the august heat wave i sway a little
while your right hand strums
and the left hand frets me
through otis redding soul
on the other end of the line

i dance alone tomorrow
to feel the wind sweep my hair
as your hands watch each other
lying curled on your thighs
awaiting a call to action
curled around barbells
forks and knives
maybe the laundry
looking for something
they can do together

the method of exit
is brutal, we say
referring to the end of days
for all of those committed alone
to hospital wards, untouchable

and think of those hands
who did not wait until they
lacked the strength
to court the end

my right hand goes on strike
for a week —
to pass the time alone
left picks up a pen
and forces unreadable letters
across the page

tonight my hands cooperate
to chop the food, shimmy the pan
while the hands of a woman
in the port of beirut
pick at the rubble
that might contain
the hands of her husband

the hands of her husband
having come to rest
cupping the back of his head
against the falling sky

while a grandmother in
the heart of lebanon sets her hands
side by side, playing auld lang syne
on the piano
amidst the debris of her ruined flat

we still find tiny occupations
for fingers, knit them together
tell them this is living now

command your hands
to set down their distractions
turn your key in my door
come hold fast to my own

this could be the last time
the silk of mine pairs yours
a cradle in a cradle
until i am only my breath
and then carried upon it
and then

may

may a white child conceived in love, grown in the country of his mother's body, who was delivered of her pain

may a white child fed from her milk, whose cheek was cradled by her hand that marveled at his softness, whose cries were tended in the night

may a white child whose shit was cleaned and scrapes were kissed and bones were mended by his mother, whose words were formed by careful repetition from her tongue, whose thoughts were so too formed, whose clothes sewn by her hand

may a white child whose games were played in the summer grass, whose questions counselled by the best of his parents' knowledge, whose family delighted in the sight of him, whose brother was consoled by his love against tyrants

may a white child who was head of his class, who was sweet on the neighbour's daughter

may a white child be raised with the warnings of his older brother who dared talk to power

may a white child dream in terror of the night they came for his grandfather, the story repeated by his ancient grandmother

may a white child, a beautiful white child, conceived
in love, grown in the country of his mother's body live
what you reject for yourself, that from which you turn
your face, live without daring to want

may a white child know that his skin is not a passport,
that his pale tint will follow him always and his
children's children

may the word of a white child count at half

may a white child's tongue struggle with the language
of thieves in vain to remember the mother tongue

may a white child never know the strength and
loveliness of his body

may a white child know better than to roam at night

may a white child thank his parents for not raising
him better

may a white child who is walking home

may a white child scream

may a white child's scream for help be unheard

may a white child's arms come down to shield his
head from a boot

may a white child who was raised to kindness lie rotting by miniscule degrees in his mother's arms freshly shot, stabbed like a bull all over the body

may a white child live long enough to see his mother's face a mask of torsion, to see the colour of his paint, to fear

may a white child, pride of his family, be remembered as their fallen hope

may a white child's name be not honoured in the evening news

may a white child die like the thousands of white children die by righteous hands each year to be forgotten in the sea of white children who constructed their own end, deserving death, reviled for their rough nature

may a white child (?)

                      (no)

may a white child (?)

                      (no)

may a white child (?)

                      (no)

why may
a black one?

cathy and heathcliffe on the moors

the signal bearers
used to come with torches
now they walk in the opposite direction
from us across the fields to meet
the doom of dying sunflowers at the farm

joyful docile not bacchanalian
holding their babies and dogs and lovers
against the backdrop of folding yellow faces
cradling sleeping bees in the evening chill

we hold each other too, amidst
the bucolic splendour of bodies reclining
on the hillocks, of burrs amongst the
overgrown rhubarbs

everyone is laughing in the high high wind
in the fading evening light
illuminated by women
in golden sundresses that outshine
the flowers turned all together
like jilted lovers in the same direction

and if it were gustier and darker
and damp, we too would be
on the untamed moors
looking for home

come, let me turn your shoulders
and console you as one
who also knows
the number of their days
and does not find ever-droll
that we live as they are dying

picking out cards in the sympathy aisle

"Your kindness the sweetest that I've ever known / Like honeycomb
holding the bee in the folds..." — *Haley Heynderickx*

the paper is double thick linen
the corners sharp on my fingers
that i lower like talia on the
wheel's flax spindle

bring nothing to suck the splinter
let me sleep a thousand years
hiding my face
with the hastily cast
thick coverlet of
mantras for lost beloveds
who *live on in memory*

i dream on my feet of hives
the well-wishing bees droning
the news amongst us
like a catching ailment
that strikes the brood uneven
so that some may recover
as others are falling
into the honeycombs
of lost dances, secrets, and toil
into pit and cradle

i am the still congregation
as the priest walks slow
between the pews, tranquilizing luban
rising at the end of the censer's
rattling chain

two other sweet wax women
coat bound, caress the cards
in their slots
waiting for the emanation
of a hot tear to soften them
murmur *excuse me*
as they reach past my body
which has failed to move

font of the covenant

i.

{enter spirit}

you folded and opened me like a rorschach parallel hoping
to discern which half might be the kinder. are those the two?
gentle and rough sisters you call upon in your dreams. i am
unsure you have learned the shapes of me. like every arabic
letter changes form subject to placement within the word. i
taste good for succour, not for scolding. how will you discover
the words to make sense of me?

{exeunt}

ii.

{loudly}

in every today i am: speaking to a czech man whose arm
　　　　　　　　　is needled with the eye of ra

　　　　　　　　　watching a woman at the fair tie a coin scarf
　　　　　　　　　on her narrow hips and shimmy
　　　　　　　　　arms raised above her
　　　　　　　　　; everybody laughs

　　　　　　　　　walking in a bleached wood in which a kemetic
　　　　　　　　　his fair flesh burnt red, holds court amidst
　　　　　　　　　the dancing witches

　　　　　　　　　lying in a meditation room
　　　　　　　　　the pyramids of giza projected on the wall
　　　　　　　　　behind the auburn-haired woman imploring me
　　　　　　　　　to imagine a glowing hand
　　　　　　　　　inviting me not into a tomb but
　　　　　　　　　the energy of the universe

　　　　　　　　　washing off the oil
　　　　　　　　　of the men who twined my hair
　　　　　　　　　in their clutching fingers, longing
　　　　　　　　　to hear me speak arabic angrily
　　　　　　　　　les reves de sauvageries romantiques
　　　　　　　　　blooming in their loins

iii.

{whispering}

at any given moment i am ready to die
as you eat a fruit i will never taste
you long to excavate
golden hued immortal fantasies
i am the curse that is coming
to put ashes in your mouth

iv.

{enter spirit}

i know the white words for the god of scribes, for wisdom and for the moon. el qamar. *wish el qamar,* you used to call me. i am trapped here a little west-born bundle ferried back and forth to the burning east to be dipped into a cistern the pictures in the desert, of everyone dressed in black but me, a little white ghost, post-font drowning and rebirth from the grave womb of a tripartite god and then where did the fathers go, and then? i was born into the light, from the womb, from the water, from the moon, from my slumber

{exeunt}

concealed weapons

i

i loved the man who called me sandn_gger
as much as the one who called me passing
too   brown for a white man /
          white for brown
but both said to me *sister*
calling down the shades
to shame me

i am tired of the men   telling me i am too angry

tired of being   the unfathomed well
                                   into which poison is poured
                                   from which sweet water hauled
                                   all the tools for boring at the ready

                                   telling me i am too tolerant
                                   of the knuckles of white girls
                                   against my body

                                   of tar tongues drawing out syllables
                                   in reply to my mother's accent

tired of those who wish   i would grind for them
                                   the earth against the sky
                                   while i am trying to live

who want   to burn up one truth
for another in their sorrow

who say   *diaspora* upon you
as casually as good morning
as knife and fork to eat you up
one morsel at a time, o where
does this little piece of you go?
be delicious, be
a joyless joan of arc in your
brownness, called
to omniscient pinnacle

taking   my trust / my money / my labour
my love / my time
never washing my dish
saying goodbye
and calling me too tolerant
and too angry

i am as lonely as you
without people

grown   alongside
lived   alongside
loved   alongside
so many   white bodies
as if to be *only*

ii

i sit inside a call to prayer, quiet like static, muted bees.
eager for the magic, to be fooled, for the flim flam. but,

                                        what is the point of that magic
                                        that transubstantiation when
the children are
aborting glitch lives
with guns in their
despair, abracadaver
now you see them, now

(when i was the sea i was gray for you and
when i was the sand i let you walk warm across my shifting back
when i was just the northern forest i was quiet and
for me alone)

                                        i have started taking pictures
                                        a catalogue: how this trick is done

first you pour the love out
then replace with fear

and if i had a gun i'd make
a parable of forgetting
in the closet of my mouth
for you

it's only you who forgets

iii

a word is an annihilator
bang
outwards then
inwards
somewhere else

really? are you really good?
really worth it?
really?

how to redeem: the lost soft love
of a really brown body
from men who really liked
the way my sandy skin
wore against their real whiteness

picture the
white police, couldn't tell me
from the jamaican boy
they called my brother
who came to lend me
the credit of a man

                    against the menace of one who said
you really are a brown bitch
i'm really going to get you

are you sure you're really
not his sister?
really muslim if arab?

how long do i have to live
in this body to be sure enough
for you?

brown girl is a weapon concealed
they think, biddable to danger
but really it's our
trampled hearts
refusing
to die
in the
blast

iv

misdirection depends
(in the photo of me
beside the white girls)
on shadow and light

here's a little
sleight of hand
where breathing fast
is rabbit's heart
finally, a drumroll

play along, sense erases
what we know
pulled from one extreme
and back, a trick of dazzle

(when i was the sea i was gray for you with worry
when i was the sand i let you knead my blood alive
when i was just the northern forest i was blackened by a fire)

other (me)
still looking
        help, i'm not just
        a woman dancing
        afraid of stopping

(when i was the sea you were concealed inside me
when i was the sand you were buried within
when i was the just northern forest you hid inside my leaves)

(i was salt and dirt in which things grew
i was the things that grew in them
i think i'll be again
i am afraid of other things than you)

i carry a weapon
concealed in my heart
that can both melt
and resist you

on the run with the cult of saint
cecilia, beheaded unrepentant

holy shit, i really
miss your squared-up shoulders
in that t-shirt that showed

you were trying to get stronger
but still had that soft
little curve to your stomach
under the muscle

so slight as not to be seen by
any eye living in a body
that had not touched you

i cannot even speak to you
have swallowed a worried tooth
its jagged edge holding the rest of me
hostage as it summers in my throat
cutting me all the way down

spilling out kensington market
of twenty years ago:
we caressed the velvet vests
and dreamed of top-hat ringmaster
courage, my love

pouring out that feeling
i'm a cherry through which
you have run the sprig of rosemary
to balance the one note of sweetness
in an otherwise unsympathetic drink

i am there, i am there
in the ghost of your unexpected
silk over steel
that is good for loving

hipiphany, legstacy
apocalips, vulvarary
the remedial cummunion

i wish you'd put your hand
in my hair again and tell me
we are soft, we are still soft

wearing this skin

wearing this skin
like a strange coat left in a frigid bar
at the end of the night
when they're taking out trash
and the back door is open
to the november air
and the ghost of old drinking
is holding my shoulder
and the ghost of old love
has an arm around my throat

wearing this skin
that's come loose from my step
so i slide on unsteady
throughout the long day
and the creases are sharper
i can't find the seams
and the small buttons multiply
in my bad dreams
take your long fingers
and open my heart
we won't call it a killing, just mercy

i am not okay
with this blatant milk kindness
salt weathers the face
leaves white accretions
under the lash line
crust in the corners

my philtrum is on fire
refraining from speaking
i went on down to the sacred well
got on my knees
and screamed all about it

i put you in the water
like a dirty dress hem
like a cry baby swaddle
like a winding cloth body
to wash you all clean
in the fear of some never
make you claw for land
but your coat sleeves are empty
and the shore's made of mud
and the tailors all know
that this coat isn't mine

hibiscus

poised over the
bone china rim
of just boiled water

flower fragrant and
so sour, it is well known
by my straight-backed
mothers, sipping
in composure
how much sugar
makes it fine

fresh vermillion upends
the sunday ladies;
how to drink
a thing inflamed
with such ill will

i suck a red drop
from my fingertip

light conversation

3,288 sparrows / or 300 books / or 1,854,759 excited bees / or

three thousand plus sparrows who hide in my wings sang me softly the reckoning of your fears and disappointments. i checked and discovered i'd be three hundred books' worth of unlearning spite for softness of limb, heat of round cheek. i would like to unleash my near two million bees' worth of stings, see if exposure leads to immunity. i'm still learning to be gracious, inside, seven million snowflakes gently falling to muffle the wrath from lax words. my heart weighs a feather. your love weighs the passing breeze. i will lose no ice. i will lose no book. i will lose no sparrow. i will lose no bee. sit with the sum of me, as i sit with your fractioned collarbone, subtracted thigh gap. if only i were made of tea, there would be 46,000 plus cups of me to sip in silence, consider the measure of how next you speak.

7,234,792 falling snowflakes / maybe also the feather of ma'at

on caressing a cool, smooth wall

i

i liked the way the
please drink responsibly
sign blurred as i gazed
from the parasol-strewn table
to the wall

you made my heart skip a beat
and took out the woman who stands
with her arms like a fortress
in front of my grief

when jane died
i walked into the tavern

they lined up the shots
i didn't speak

ii

i liked the way your mouth tasted
as we made bad decisions

but the waking was rough

dearest, it's tomorrow that we fear

what is the half-life of hope?
the event horizon of joy?

the sleeper waits for us to join
at the bottom of the bottle

iii

i remember the night
we set the kitchen on fire
for a moment
with the cognac
we were using to flambé
and swirled like silent birds
putting out the flames
before anyone could wake

iv
(for r.mclennan)

at the carleton tavern
though stephen was late
and ruth already reading
you stole a wineglass
from the unattended bar
and poured him a beer
from your pitcher —
this was love

at d'arcy mcgees
at a tiny round table
barely enough to hold
our half-full amber glasses
my tears of frustration fell
barefaced and ugly —
this was love

no green shirt complete
without a bottle of beer
cresting the pocket
as i repaired your glasses at the bar
so you could get on stage —
this was love

the night i met you
strangling stems of empty wineglasses
you condemned to the road
from the second floor balcony
where we spoke —
this was love

you write "hero"
on letters destined for my door
and though i wait to feel strong
i know this love

v

i miss the flask so round
and polished

passed at the fire
from my hand to yours

tip yourself one communion
with your brothers

tip yourself a toast
with the writers

tip yourself a slap in the mouth
to break the longest day

vi

how short, everything
on this planet
of green dragontail butterfly
and self-annihilating monkey tribes
cross-species collaborative
dreams of colonies in the stars
of magic and chemistry
in a shot glass
of mutual hallucination

let us sweeten the story

my eye is not diluted
by the drink

let me measure with my finger
how deep our mistakes may be tonight

let me love the shine on your cheek
and the miracle of your pupil
softly expanding in the light

i could not sing
and you sent me songs
tones rounded by
the aged oak barrels

i could not feel
and you brought me
the automatic drum
of your body to remind me

vii

the hazy woman
reflected in the window
looks mean

i think i love her
i think she
doesn't wait around
i think she
takes her own opinion

all of a sudden
i forget how to swallow
i open my mouth and
cold drink tilts in
my throat shut against it
no. nothing. nothing else

yeah, i say. *it's good,* i say
i feel good
par for the course
hoping you don't
know what that means

see? even poison
can be funny

tokyo cinema

tonight i want to hear no sound
that is not your heart
or your sated sigh
as i hold you
in the
dark
surrounded
by strangers
and kiss the skin
that holds your sadness

why have we never
been so tender and so quiet

even once fine machines
will break their gears
murmur down into stillness

the soundless scene
in every film
builds tension

let's dissolve into
silken inner elbows
unwrapped collarbones
and the texture of a cheek
as perceived by calm fingers

i have stopped recording my dreams
in a book for they are all the same
dream where we are sitting at a table
in the homes askew where i grew up
and i am feeding you or you are feeding me
the home food of our ancestors
from across the middle-east and we
are crying, we are crying, with our faces
in our hands for this meal will never be perfect
and i cannot cook the rice your mother made
as you cannot cook the rice of mine, but the music
of the meal in our mouths is so close
and recalls what we have lost, and our tears
become our salt, each according to their need
and i cannot hold you, as i cannot judge you
for wanting to drown the world under your hand
in the darkness of your grief

the shoe of the dervish
that is the path to ecstasy
knows only spin and pressure
creating its own dust in the wear

Some poems in this collection have appeared previously in the following publications:

"bird's tongue" appeared in *In/Words, Issue 17.2 – Food Issue*, February 2018.

"peremptory challenge" appeared in the *In/Words special issue dis(s)ent*, 2018.

"syrian aperture" appeared in *Canthius, Issue 4*, 2017, and online http://www.canthius.com/feed-1/2018/3/8/four-poems-by-natalie-hanna.

"white coat" appeared in the chapbook *concealed weapons/animal survivors*, 2018.

"may" appeared in the chapbook *dark ecologies, 2017*.

"font of the covenant" will appear in the above/ground press publication, *touch the donkey*, October 2020.

"concealed weapons" appeared in the chapbook *concealed weapons/ animals survivors*, 2018 and on the pomeleon web site, 2018: http://www.poemeleon.org/natalie-hanna/.

"on the run with the cult of saint cecilia, beheaded unrepentant" appeared in the above/ground press publication, *touch the donkey*, October 2020.

A differently formatted version of "light conversation" won Honourable Mention in *ARC Poetry Magazine*'s Diana Brebner prize 2019, and also appeared in *ARC 91:Spring Issue*, 2020.

"tokyo cinema" appeared in *Vallum - Home issue 17:1* as digital content: https://www.vallummag.com/current_issue.html

Transliterated words/phrases

Alhamdullilah – praise be to God
ana mish ayza akol lisan al'asfour – i don't want to eat the
    bird's tongue (a name for orzo)
asafeer 'il – birds, the
bukra – tomorrow
galabeya – a loose fitting kaftan-like garment
halawa – a kind of sugar wax
il ingilisi – English
il' asafeer – the birds
imbarrih – yesterday
Inshallah – if God wills it
kinisa – church
kolli, ya albi – eat, oh my heart
kolli ya habibti, kolli – eat, oh my love, eat
lisan al'asfour – the tongue of the bird (the bird's tongue)
Masr – Egypt
mish oulini ya om'mi, fi eh? – not tell me mother, what's wrong
naharda – today
rashwa – bribery
ya rab – oh God

Notes

1 On January 4, 2022, after I had written this poem, I learned of Marwa
Helal's poem "Poem to be read to Right to Left," in a style she created
called The Arabic. (http://www.wintertangerine.com/helal-poem-to-
be-read) It was a joyful, transformative moment to see another poet had
identified a need for a form that flips the concept of Second Languages.

2 R v Kent, (1986), 40 Man. R. (2d) 160, (1986) 27 CCC (3d) 405 (Man. C.A.)
at p. 421. "An accused has no right to demand that members of his race
be included on the jury. To so interpret the Charter would run counter
to Canada's multicultural and multiracial heritage and the right of
every person to serve as a juror". R v Pan, 2014 ONSC 1393 at para 31,
R v. Kokopenance (ONCA) at para 26. A representative jury is important
as it "contributes to a sense of confidence that the jury will be fair and
impartial." A representative jury has the effect of bringing a diversity of
backgrounds and experiences, in addition to cultural sensitivities.

3 I.e. in 2016, an Ottawa police officer pled guilty to making racist online
comments that perpetuated the myth of the "drunken indian," in
relation to the death of renowned Inuk artist, Annie Pootoogook.
http://www.cbc.ca/news/canada/ottawa/ottawa-police-racist-
comments-1.3831028.

The words "starlight tour" refer to the practice of police of driving
Indigenous persons to remote, frozen, locations and leaving them there,
sometimes resulting in their deaths. See Maclean's coverage, "New light
on Saskatoon's 'starlight tours.' http://www.macleans.ca/news/canada/
new-light-on-saskatoons-starlight-tours/.

See Shakespeare, *Hamlet* Act I, Scene 5.

4 Peregrin praetor, "Foreigner judge," the Roman concept of a judge to
handle suits between parties where one or both are "foreigners."

In the trial for the death of Colten Boushie, the jury that rendered the
acquittal (with second degree murder and manslaughter being possible
outcomes) heard statements that the accused was allegedly fearful,
defending against theft, and did not intend harm. To acquit, the
jury needed to find his actions were reasonable. *The Toronto Star*,
"A look at the evidence the jury considered in the Gerald Stanley

murder trial." https://www.thestar.com/news/canada/2018/02/13/a-look-at-the-evidence-the-jury-considered-in-the-gerald-stanley-murder-trial.html.

5 The initial Freedom Convoy occupation of Ottawa, ostensibly for the purpose of protesting government COVID policies affecting the livelihood of participants, was reported to be at least partially arranged by people with links to far-right hate groups, and attracted this element to the event. This event, widely condemned by the residents of Ottawa, both in the immediately affected area and beyond, has spurned Civil law suits, criminal charges, distrust in the local police, and was punctuated by and was punctuated by reports of assaults and harassment, some of which may qualify for investigation as hate-based, that weigh heavy on the city's collective memory.

This poem is imagined as a response in conversation with the various young, white men who wished to convince me that there was nothing untoward that could be associated with the event, not to be afraid, and that in their experiences of being at the event (as white men interested in discoursing with participants or as direct participants), everyone was cordial and welcoming. This poem expresses the maelstrom of ideas I could not reply with in the moment.

I would urge readers to review Tanya Talaga's piece in *The Globe and Mail*, "There have always been two Canadas. In this reckoning on racism, both must stand together for Indigenous people now," published on June 12 (and updated on June 16) 2020. https://www.theglobeandmail.com/opinion/article-there-have-always-been-two-canadas-in-this-reckoning-on-racism-both/.

In speaking about the principle of "Two Canadas" (one for non-Indigenous and one for Indigenous people) Talaga comments: "Canada's unique brand of racism can be quiet and loud. It manifests as indifference and it has crept into all public institutions, government agencies, corporations and in the way you look away from the homeless Indigenous man you see sitting on the sidewalk." Bias and racism are insidious, and require concerted effort to unlearn, including recognizing that the lived experiences of people different from you have shaped their worldview, and that just because you have not lived those same experiences, does not mean they do not exist.

Acknowledgements

This book is dedicated to my family, Mona Akoury and Nancy Hanna, and to R.B. Fairchild, Tamara Fairchild, Diana Reid, Lisa Reid, and Elizabeth Reid for making me a part of their families. Without their unfailing faith and support I would not have become the person, author, or lawyer I am today.

Particular thanks are extended to the following people:

To Janet Cover, for being the kind of English teacher every child needs, without whom I would not have imagined success.
To rob mclennan, for championing me always.
To Liam Burke, for returning the words, for which I remain in glad debt.
To Jennifer Pederson and Sunny Marriner, in strength and solidarity, for the rest of our days.

My profound thanks and respect to Andy Verboom, Jacqueline Valencia, and Annick MacAskill, for their principled ethics and for reading and supporting earlier versions of this manuscript.

My very deepest thanks to Irene Bindi for her excellent editorial eye, and to Todd Besant for giving this collection a beautiful home with ARP Books. It has been a sincere pleasure.

In over twenty-five years of writing, there are countless current and former members of the Ottawa (and environs) literary (and music) community to thank for hosting me, for collaboration, and for instruction, mentorship, and advice. These include rob mclennan, Jennifer Pederson, Sanita Fejzić, Conyer Clayton, Nathanaël Larochette, Manahil Bandukwala, Stephen Brockwell, Avonlea Fotheringham, VERSeFest, Aella, Ellen Chang-Richardson, nina jane drystek, Margo LaPierre, LM Rochefort, Danielle K.L. Gregoire, Cameron Anstee, Jennifer Baker, Marilyn Irwin, Shery Alexander Heinis, Monty Reid, Jeff Blackman, Jessica Ruano, Marilyn Irwin, Chris Johnson, Rusty Priske, Claire Farley, Chuqiao Yang, Pearl Pirie, Cathy and Steve Zytveld, AJ Dolman, Amanda Earl, Christine McNair, Stuart Ross, Amanda Cottreau, Frances Boyle, Apollo the Child, Jamaal Jackson Rogers, Deanna Young, and Jason Sonier, *but to name a few.* The list is truly endless. All of our interactions have made me immeasurably richer, and I am grateful.

natalie hanna is an Ottawa lawyer of Middle-Eastern descent, working with low income populations. Her writing focusses on feminist, political, and personal relational themes. She has been a past Administrative Director of the Sawdust Reading Series and past board member of *Arc Poetry Magazine*. Her poetry and reviews have appeared in print and online in Canada and the U.S. Her poem "light conversation" received Honourable Mention in *ARC Magazine*'s 2019 Diana Brebner Prize. She is the author of twelve poetry chapbooks, including titles with above/ground press and Baseline Press, and the co-author, with Liam Burke, of *machine dreams* with Collusion Books. *lisan al'asfour* is her first full length collection.